more praise for
DOWN THE FOGGY STREET OF MY MIND

"A melancholic poetic tapestry of memory and trauma and the feminist fight to rise above it."

Koraly Dimitriadis
author of *Just Give Me The Pills*
and *Love and F**ck Poems*

"This is a collection that wraps the mind around a journey replete with bravery. It is an intricate look at how to navigate the waters of trauma. The poetry in this manuscript faces the many truths society too often turns away from, and leads the reader to 'see the forest beyond.' 'Breathing here takes practice' as the poet tells us, through each and every stanza.

These poems open our eyes to importance of the flick of a light switch, the sideways drift of tires, crows and oak trees, and a dog that softly snores on a train. Parker is a poet who mends and sews the poems of healing. She helps us to understand 'trauma is like that, missing pieces, filled in, stitched together like a quilt.' "

Connie Post
author of *Floodwater* and *Prime Meridian*

"Unsettled, in her own word: unrelenting. In *Down the Foggy Streets of my Mind* Kelliane Parker constructs a reverse geometric proof of home. The she in the poems runs, flys, makes plans, inhabits women's culture and makes a home out of abstracted stories and women's culture. These poems are uneasy, fretful and they have town edges. If it's not you it's someone you know, and these poems are an escape map to a different sense of self."

Kim Shuck
7th Poet Laureate of San Francisco

"In Kelliane Parker's new book, Down the Foggy Streets of my Mind: Portal to Dissociation, we travel with her into the depths of her soul to find 'the trauma underground', where 'the only escape is past fear.' We are taken on a painfully authentic journey where secrets are revealed, and past abuses are exposed through poems that are raw and uncompromising. As a survivor, Kelliane searches for a safe spot within herself, and encourages us to do the same. During her remarkable journey inward, she writes poems of despair, but also ones that honor the strength of her wise women ancestors, and the healing powers of nature. Read these amazing poems of resilience, and learn what it means to finally be able to reclaim one's own life."

Johanna Ely
6th Poet Laureate of Benicia

NOMADIC PRESS

OAKLAND

111 FAIRMONT AVENUE
OAKLAND, CA 94611

BROOKLYN

475 KENT AVENUE #302
BROOKLYN, NY 11249

WWW.NOMADICPRESS.ORG

MASTHEAD

FOUNDING PUBLISHER
J. K. FOWLER

ASSOCIATE EDITOR
MICHAELA MULLIN

EDITOR
MK CHAVEZ

DESIGN
JEVOHN TYLER NEWSOME

MISSION STATEMENT

Through publications, events, and active community participation, Nomadic Press collectively weaves together platforms for intentionally marginalized voices to take their rightful place within the world of the written and spoken word. Through our limited means, we are simply attempting to help right the centuries' old violence and silencing that should never have occurred in the first place and build alliances and community partnerships with others who share a collective vision for a future far better than today.

INVITATIONS

Nomadic Press wholeheartedly accepts invitations to read your work during our open reading period every year. To learn more or to extend an invitation, please visit: www.nomadicpress.org/invitations

DISTRIBUTION

Orders by teachers, libraries, trade bookstores, or wholesalers:

Nomadic Press Distribution
orders@nomadicpress.org
(510) 500-5162
nomadicpress.org/store

Small Press Distribution
spd@spdbooks.org
(510) 524-1668 / (800) 869-7553

Cover art: Arthur Johnstone

Published by Nomadic Press, 111 Fairmount Avenue, Oakland, California 94611

First printing, 2022

Library of Congress Cataloging-in-Publication Data

Title: *Down the Foggy Streets of My Mind: Portal to Dissociation*
p. cm.
Summary: *Down The Foggy Streets Of My Mind: Portal to Dissociation*, is an ode to those of us who live with Dissociative Disorders such as PTSD and DID. It is an unapologetic anthem for survivors of sexual violence to rid themselves of being shamed and blamed in silence. When we tell our truth, we take back our power, as powerlessness lives in hiding.

[1. POETRY / Subjects & Themes / Mental Health. 2. POETRY / Subjects & Themes / LGBTQIA+. 3. POETRY / Subjects & Themes / Women Authors. 4. POETRY / American / Latinx. 5. POETRY / American / General.] I. III. Title.

LIBRARY OF CONGRESS CONTROL NUMBER: 2021949440

ISBN: 978-1-955239-14-1

DOWN THE FOGGY STREETS OF MY MIND

PORTAL TO DISSOCIATION

KELLIANE PARKER

DOWN THE FOGGY STREETS OF MY MIND

PORTAL TO DISSOCIATION

KELLIANE PARKER

NOMADIC PRESS

CONTENTS

introduction

reading guide

INTRODUCTION

Welcome to my journey, there is hope on the other side of hiding, something I did for 25 years. During that time, I told no one about my diagnosis, I was terrified of what would happen if anyone found out. Living with a diagnosis of DID, (at the time referred to as Multiple Personality Disorder in 1991), was both liberating and terrifying. Liberating because I learned that I wasn't crazy, something that I secretly feared. And terrifying because I was afraid that people around me, who thought I was strong and solid would now think I was crazy.

This book was written first to save myself and now to help others. The first step on this healing journey was to accept that there was no such thing as normal, and to stop hiding. Societal norms of western culture dictate a rigid and narrow confine of what to fit our unique selves into. And then we wonder why we lack self worth. We are told that if we don't fit into these neat little boxes that we are flawed and undesirable.

When I met my first therapist, she was a Psychology PhD candidate whose research was about new therapies for those with Multiple Personality Disorder. She was partnered with another PhD candidate who was focused on Borderline Personality Disorder. They put together a group therapy of women who had experienced early, long term extreme sexual abuse, knowing that they could find subjects for their research. It worked, and I was selected to be a research subject. For most of the 6 years

we worked together, I met with my therapist two three hour sessions per week. It saved my life.

Prior therapies for these types of disorders focused on reconditioning the pathologized mind. This new work, instead used a form of family therapy, Internal Family Systems, that is now widely used. At the time it was considered radical and those before me were sometimes subjected to shock therapy or worse. The idea was, just like people work on nurturing their inner child, someone with DID would nurture and communicate with inner children or selves. As my therapy progressed I began to live my life not totally numb.

We have in our so-called ideal of normalcy an acceptance of inner lives, inner selves and an inner child. This idea is mainstream and widely accepted. But the notion of someone having more than one self, and that those others, (my system abhors the word alters), may have separate feelings or sense of self is considered aberrant. This myth has been perpetuated by the media, literature and movies.

The truth is that people like me work very hard to fit in. We are scapegoated as being the very definition of crazy. That is the biggest myth I am working to dispel. The thought of putting this in writing for all the world to see, terrified me. And yet, I knew I had to do it, I am no longer in hiding and I will no longer tolerate blame, shame and stigma. In fact, being a multiple comes with its own gifts, many with DID have a wide range of unique talents. Something that most singletons don't share the same breadth.

DOWN THE FOGGY STREETS OF MY MIND 1

You will find the trauma underground
The only escape is past the fear
Through murkiness
Bumping into sharp edges
Clinging to the building
On narrow ledge
And once inside
Run down the stairs
To find passage to the other side
Turn the page
To find the door

WHILE THE WORLD SLEEPS

I negotiate and wrestle
Let go and become
The night person
Sleepless
Untamed and improper
Irreverent and unmanageable
Unpredictable and uncooperative
I unearth secrets
And deconstruct stories
Lies carefully crafted and rehearsed
By the entire cast
In the role of a lifetime
For a lifetime
A life sentence, really
I nurture and embrace
The Survivor
Who faced down monsters
From untold fairy tales
Where the rest of the world
Finds us unworthy
Of being saved or believed
So again we save ourselves
Unless we don't

And then the body goes uncounted
By the unspeakable cancer called shame
And another is lost
And, another...is... lost
So, tell me your secrets
The truths you don't even tell yourself
What could you lose?
To tell another unworthy
The familiar tale
Only the cast member names are different
But the story is the same
So we share the secret handshake
To acknowledge our membership
Only this time, it is different
We are the majority
And the light no longer stings our eyes
Or maybe it makes us feel alive
To feel something, anything
Even pain is beautifully real
You, my sisters, count
I see you, I hear you
I remember your name
And I, I believe you

WHAT DO YOU CALL HOME?

They say you can never go back home
For me that is very true
For home to me was not a place, but a person
A humble, modest living person

Her name was Lupe Teresa Mesa
Mi abuelita, my grandmother
For whom my daughter's middle name is Lupita
The woman who prayed the rosary and walked everywhere
Who taught ESL and volunteered at church and library

Lupe Theresa Mesa was the richest woman in the world
and meant it, not rich in things
As a widow who raised her children and orphaned nephews
A 3 bedroom, 2 bath in Panorama City
Perfect for a family of 14

A house full of happy noises
The sound of guitars and song, of poetry read
A crowd of people bursting out of every room, all busy following
their passions
Heated political debates in the living room, cooking and laughter
in the kitchen

All orbiting in the spell of this tiny, center of our universe

She kept me from floating into nothingness
She tethered me to Earth
I thought her strong, solid...permanent
Had I known it how tenuous it was, I would have skipped work
For one more chance to sit at her kitchen table, her alter of magic
Where a cup of tea, stories of the family and folklore
Would transport me in a magic carpet ride

I cling to traces of her, like rose-scented lotion
I hold her rosary, the one with the tiny magnified picture
Nuestra Senora, for whom she was named
And now I grasp at any detail, like the sound of her laugh
To will back the feel of her hands clasping mine

I close my eyes and smell hibiscus flowers, taste their nectar
Imagine the cactus that climbed the stucco and the hummingbirds that nested there
The giant oak tree I used to climb and flock of parrots that roosts there still
And the lone cockatoo who would rather be a parrot, than be alone
How they would circle at dusk and settle in the tree and make a ruckus
The neighbors were not fans, but she loved them, so I did too

I remember how they fell instantly silent when the sun was gone
Like the flick of a light switch
And now that switch has darkened the window and obscured my view
From the person for whom I once called home

INSTRUCTIONS: TO INSULATE FROM MOONLIGHT

Instructions to insulate from moonlight
Wear malachite, drink hawthorn berries
Prepare for the next cycle
In the infinite loop

Remember to breathe
As the sun starts to fade
And paints clouds from below
While anxiety grows into a flower named dread

Snapping photos to steal light
Which I hide in my pocket
To later conjure safety
But land eludes me

I begin pacing in a rhythm
This is the dance of my culture
This is the dance of my youth
While my feet lift off the ground

And so I float and spin

With no handhold in sight
No means to make it stop
Until I'm swept up in the current

Then the images come
First, like faded super 8
Flash hyper-sensory, then de-sensory fog
That tastes of bile and rot

It slowly slows
The nauseating spinning
Rapid flipping
Familiar state of dissociation

Of familiar tasks that elude me
Like opening doors
So I wait, I wait before them
Until memory returns

After running from this burning building of a body
Avoiding mirrors to evade
The reflection of wild-eyed-animal-eye-shine

The familiar and the totem
And nothing
Then the nothing
The welcoming, familiar nothing
Weighty- blanket of nothing

And I return
Time lost, but grateful
I have survived another
Until next...full moon

THE DAY I STOPPED FEELING

I'm suffocating
Under the weight of male hatred
And you want something from me that does not belong to you
Something that you don't really want
But to consume, destroy, to annihilate
And on that day, the day I stopped feeling
The sun still shone brightly as if it didn't know
And I never saw it coming
To be taken to the lake by a stranger and wonder
Is this the end of my life, or just my living
There is this brief moment in time between the belief that
everything will be ok
And the horrifying moment that your greatest fears are just about
to come true...
And then I'm left alone, with the one who will annihilate
While the other is paid with a bottle of alcohol
As if that is the fucking going rate for a person's humanity
And for me it was, my worth traded for drunkenness
And I try to hang on to myself
Like how is this happening
And my head smacking against the window
But I... I'm not really there

You see, it was not the first, but it was the worst
It was the day I stopped feeling for many years
I sat back and watched as the last fragile part of myself
Was slammed to the ground and shattered into a million unfixable shards
And a part of me, celebrated
As you can ONLY be reduced to shards but once
Victimhood slowly loses its grip of power
Until it becomes a nuisance
I remember a time, early on
When I spent days, smoking cigarettes
Trying to pass the vast emptiness
Created by your contact with me
Long after the blood washed away and bruises faded
And here I sit, one of an army of robots
Created by your belief that ANYTHING about YOU matters
IT. DOES. NOT. You are worthless
You are unnecessary
And yet the FUCKING world values your opinion over mine
And as I choose to leave this life as a robot... a zombie
 I must take back what's mine
That is the unreachable part of me that you never touched

And say
That you are not here
You were never here

AT THE MOMENT OF IMPACT

You see but can't stop it
Can't stop the inevitable impact
So you brace yourself
Count seconds that feel like hours
Hours of countdown
Until impact
Inevitable impact
With forces unstoppable
Like Newton's law
And so great, to take down light poles
Take down walls, smash windows, crush doors
That sideways drift of tires
Tires smoking, rubber burning
Resisting loss of control
Sideways careening
Before impact
Inevitable impact
Shrill of crystalline glass explosion
Before dull thud against metal
And those inside who don't survive
Despite seatbelts and airbags
Breathing but long dead

Warm shell, long dead
Long gone, but breathing
Pulse and heartbeat
But dead, just the same
She left this world
Before she started
When it was etched into her being
Re-written in her DNA
A stain unremovable
And so indelible
Only suns of millennia
Will bleach it from her bones
So she leaves the form
The tainted self, scarred body
And stands just outside
Out of reach
Out of touch
Untouchable
Unfindable
Where she braces
And waits for...
Impact

FLASHBACK

When I close my eyes the images come
They are why I wait past midnight
To brave yes, brave sleep
For sleep offers no relief
Flashes like rapid slaps
Stinging my soul
Sometimes in a trickle
But then in a flood
Relics, and faces upon faces and faces
Or slick, coppery pools of blood
Counterintuitively I open my eyes
To block out the torrent
And the light makes them fade
I cling to the light like a life raft
Sometimes the stabbing pain in my side
Or the whirring sound of a bathroom fan
Attacking senses on all sides
And so vivid, brighter than so called reality
Til the reptilian brain lashes out and flees
Against some so-called mythological predator
Only I can see
Only I can smell

Only I can hear
Only I can feel
Only I
Can't make it stop

THE CRUEL TIME MACHINE

We filter through ash and ruin
Relics from our past
Reminders of another time ?
We cannot we let go

We shed the past, as molted skin
We leave in shambles
Detritus of our past
Which deserves no name
Or acknowledgement?

Searching for answers
That don't make sense
But anger and confuse
And leave more questions

Remembering what we can't remember
Talisman of remembrance
Symbol of memory, hieroglyph
Ethereal and ambiguous

You can't interpret a singular language
Made for one, so alien
Unfamiliar with human custom
Like regret or empathy

And yet return again and again
Going back into the rubble
Trying to salvage heirlooms
Of an invented memory

Pushing aside the truth
Truth you have been avoiding
But instead return to the past
Family-run revisionist history

Collective denial with lone dissenter
Rogue dissenter is discredited
Until now, she pushes back
Not needing validation

They would rather sacrifice her
Than expose the tumor
The one who eats children

A hunger so unquenchable

That generations long after

Will know his finest pupils

Who will feed them grenades

THE ABYSS

It is a beautiful day, only you aren't part of any of it

I see you contemplating the water's edge and you begin to walk slowly
out into the water

I watch at first unconcerned, then I hold my breath and wait for what
I know is coming

You walk slowly, intentionally, not stopping, until you pass the first
and then second break

I start yelling, telling you not to go out any further
but you aren't listening

You just keep moving farther away from shore, until a large wave grabs
you and pulls you further out

And I'm yelling for help and people jump in and paddle out

And I swim to where you are and you go under just before I reach you,
but you don't fight it

This strange force pulls me down too. I fight and struggle to get to you

And the bubbles go up toward the light to freedom

But you and I? We just keep going down, down, down into the abyss

Where the light starts to fades and the sound is muffled

I try to reach you, but you just give me that look that says, it's too hard

And my lungs feel like they are going to burst, but all I see in you
 is resignation

But I won't stop, I can't stop, I won't

And the bubbles go up toward the light to freedom
But you and I, we keep going down, down, down to the abyss
Where the light is just a speck at the surface and all I hear are the
sounds of my own struggle
And the rescuers busy themselves in a flurry of activity at the surface
And I, I negotiate with god, trading everything to bring you back
And the bubbles go up toward the light to freedom
But you and I, you and I, you and I
Don't

THE VOICES OF
MY ANCESTORS

It is a casual conversation
Between the hummingbird and I
The cheerful scolding, I enjoy
Oh the crow has his opinions
I give full audience to his complaints
The crow, my fellow traveler
The turkey vulture, my guide
The parrot, my grandmother
The oak trees, my roots
Anchored deeply into golden hills
These living phoenixes
Are cleansed by the sun
To protect me from night
We talk, all day and night
The voices of my ancestors
Talking and singing
Cooking and creating
My grandma Lupe stirs the pot
She holds my hand, stirs and hums
The smell of lemon tea
The sound of slippers shuffling

Are to me the sound of safety
And I found entry
In the in-between space
This space of invisibility
Where I am not alone
An astral traveler
Here, welcome resident
Outside the busyness of business
I convene with the dead
To see them you must slow down
Step off, let go
Here you have to listen
Here there is no status quo
Death is the beautiful equalizer
Of a Venn diagram of then and now
Here green paper means nothing
Back in the eternal
I am the conduit
If you want to find home
Find your ancestors
Look into my eyes
And ask your question

SKY SALUTE

The vacant eyes reflect nothing
Absorbs all light
Nothing escapes when gaze locks
That tractor beam of imminent doom
Frozen limbs and forgotten voice
The endless seconds of slow motion
Go on forever, way too fast
The urge to fight or flee
Is answered with paralysis
As I watch the red nocturnal bloom
Eating flower after flower of tropical shirt.
He wobbles unsteadily
Gaze too unfixed
And crumbles to asphalt.
And the bright flashes of sting
Let a little life out with every sky salute

INTO THE FOG

This place I know
Where humanity is left behind
The body cannot live here
Here there is only being
Some call it Zen
Just breathing in and out
Breathing takes practice
For those new here
This is where I call home
Where I've lived longer than anywhere else
The deeper I go in
The safer it feels
Back to the dark corners
Where solid walls insure
Two directions of security
Under invisibility cloak
I sink in and rest
I breathe in and out
Lenses fogged and grey
The velvet air of nothingness
Effortlessness and floating
Embraced by quiet anonymity

This is the trauma underground
This is the in between
The place to flee the body
Discard it and run
Run until you can fly
Fly until you can float
The place I feel safe
Because here there be no monsters
Here monsters are afraid
Of being gutted or burned
And so they should
This lawless place of survivors
Has very lenient courts
When the fuse of years
Explodes fire and shrapnel
The vigilantes
Know every road
Every turn
We run scenarios
And make plans

WHEN BRAVERY CRUMBLES

Exposing something amorphous
Of the oyster or clam
Woven delicate threads
Snaking into softness,
holding, Furiously holding
Desperately holding, Tenuously
holding, Then the tiny pings
Off the rupture of each string
Broken harp strings
One by one they snap
The tinny squeals
Cattle prods the nerves, the core
Panic, as you desperately
Try to piece together
Broken china shards of bravery
Glued back together
Again and again, broken
Cubist broken
Kintsugi broken
Wabi Sabi broken
The solid looking wall
Never more than a facade

More smooth than sturdy
More hard than strong
More to hold liquid, than lava
With fractured mirrors
To hide and distort
To keep you inside
Inside and protected
Walled inside
Walled away
Walled away
And beautifully broken

7 TRUTHS AND THE LIES

First Truth, a knight in shining armor has never been to battle
In fact, there is no honor in sending others to die on your behalf
Or in the name of god or goddess
If the heavens wanted them
They would quietly scoop them up
Enfold them in their arms
Take them to them afterworld
Like they do every day, no theatrics needed

The lie is that man is king of his castle
This binary contract needs rewriting
Second Truth, the queens of the castle
Are the real heroes in this story
Wanna hear a true fairy tale?
Where the woman sweats and tolls, alone
And turns cobwebs into dinner
Turns rags into blankets and sheds into homes
Burns cascara sagrada to conjure missing coins
Coins that hobble together just enough

The Third Truth, she keeps it to herself
Her children never really know

Just how close to the edge they've lived
Forth Truth, she has magic
Given from grandmother, to mother to daughter
From all the women before
The teas when you are sick
Art and music for the soul
Dancing in the living room
Humming and dancing in the kitchen
The recipes peppered with humming
The dish not right without it

Truth Five? There is power and healing
Power and healing in a garden
The gardener plants themselves in soil
To regenerate and heal
Waters the earth with sweat
And a few drops of blood
Truth Six, the sewing needle
Nearly everything can be repaired
With shaky, wrinkled hands
That wield a needle like a sword
The tear threaded with stories

Stories of strength and endurance

And the lie is that we are not enough
That women need a provider, breadwinner
When we have always been the provider
The safe place for a baby to begin life and feed
The Seventh Truth is this
When I was lost, with no material means
My ancestors told me, you are free

I asked how I would feed my children?
Patiently they reminded me of my gifts
My wealth of things immaterial
A stitch, a garden, a poem or song
And kneaded together with love, like dough
Slowly, with joy and gratitude

WHEN I WAS 10

I was hit by a car
I don't remember being hit
That part is blank
But I heard a car behind me
I turned just in time to see it
And seconds or minutes later
I woke in a heap in the gutter
I was tangled up in my bike
My chin scraped bloody from hitting the curb
My straight teeth now crooked
A spot scraped bald on my scalp
Rained blood that blurred my vision
My wrists cut up
It would take a hospital visit
To find I had whiplash
Adrenaline and shock
Made me impervious to my plight
Unaware of any injury
I only had one thought
Get home
Only near the middle of the block
The more I walked the farther away home seemed

And my bike seemed to roll effortlessly
As I walked it back home
Until I collapsed on the not-quite-shut, front door
And fell in the entryway

There my sister screamed
When she saw me in an injured pile
Crumpled on the floor
My bike wheel bent and unmoving
Like me
Trauma is like that
Missing pieces, filled in
Stitched together like a quilt
Stitched with threads of both obligation and freedom
It isn't pretty or comforting
To wear trauma is to have more questions
To feel at ease with that unease
And the best that you can hope for
Is to know and admit
To scorch shame with healing sunlight
To save yourself
Even if you have to leave others behind

Those that won't step into the light
Too ashamed, too afraid
Trapped in Stockholm Syndrome
Where freedom is behind a door
A door always unlocked
Unlocked but forbidden
So most wait
Wait for permission that will never come
Permission to know the worst of humanity
And then keep moving

I, THE LIVING FRACTAL

As it reaches through the earth
To swallow and obliterate
To consume and erase
I keep close, in view of
The Hydra of my daydreams
Resides in no watery grave
But everywhere after dark
In the eye of the storm
Such safe insulation
From the winds of violence
Let free the satellites
Chosen cautiously, consciously
As if cradled into orbit
Who dare pass
The Rings of Saturn
The Moons of Jupiter
So meteor scarred
Rings worth the price
of the protection they afford
Where outside
Blades of saws torment
Invisible helixes held within

The vacuum permits not light
But only aquatic sounds, like blood
Pulsing in ears and chest
Entrenched in solitude

The sturdy wall of chaos
Random like wildflowers
While the artist befriends madness

MELANCHOLY

Melancholy is not sadness
But only a taint, a very faint stain
A hint of sorrow not quite there
But there nonetheless
A lingering dull ache
A hollow place inside
As familiar as a friend
A friend who doesn't bring good news
But has a realness around it
As if it were a solid state
You could throw your arms around
But is and isn't there

Real as water, real as earth
Though not made of the earth
But levitating delicately defying gravity
Real as gravity, sure as gravity
Sure as the moon
And almost too far to touch
But there
There just the same
As constant as you can count on

As you embrace and can be embraced by melancholy
Wrap it close to your skin and breathe it in deeply
Welcome its companionship

WE MEET OURSELVES ALONG THE WAY
(Impersonating Color)

Houseplant now bored and ignored,
No longer green as spring
But greying, melancholy green
Resigned to root bound subsistence
Restrained into merely existence
No longer lives up to living

Like yellow, arctic sun
Who feigns warmth, but only polishes ice
Into frozen crystal prison,
Immortalized for eternity
Stops time, but not the wanting
Wanting for warmth and
Freedom from the permafrost

Like sparkling rainbow promise
Shimmering distant mirage
Only discover on closer look
A neon reality, without air

Without trees or flowers
Only harsh assault to eyes and soul
Only this for that, knowing that you'll pay too much

But freedom is worth the overcharge
Worth the bankruptcy
Worth poverty and ruin
Material things have no value here
Your money's no good here
Here we shed toxicity, exhale stale air
Shed the physical body and world

We return and repose on soil
We tell the earth our truth,
Reveal the lies and secrets
And she embraces us
As we unfold and take root here
The next chapter appears to us
And we are welcomed home.

STRESS

Dog bark grating
I don't know
Will you stop asking what's for dinner?

Bills piled up
Who gets paid?
I don't care, I don't care

Making schedules
I don't know
Will you stop asking
Figure it out for yourself

Raising voices
I can't hear you
Don't talk louder
I will mute you

People overload
Will you stop asking?
I can't keep smiling
If I don't care

Voices louder
So incessant
Will you stop asking
I don't have all the answers

Heart is pounding
I can't sleep
Can't stop pacing
Can't stop thinking

Dog bark questions
I don't care
So don't keep asking
I need to clear my head!

OBLIGATIONS OF PHYSICAL LAW

In my quiet, dark place
No sound breaks
A still, familiar haunt
No doors permitted, lest the solitude be broken
Compelling feeling, I must overcome
Desire overpowers
Shall I faint or conquer
Will it satisfy or crush me
Can I live without it?
Silence broken
Do I choose to hear the sound?
Or do my ears have some obligation to physical law
When the light rushes in
Can I push it out again?
When it ceases to warm me
Refuses to touch me
The wanting going into uncertainty

MORNING MISSION MUSINGS

Today I wandered the Mission District in San Francisco. I watched as construction people furiously polished it to a shine. It made me reflect on where the people go? The ones who were never new and shiny, where do they go now? Those gritty, city folk who were born with old souls and world-weary eyes, what now? The ones whose faces are freckled with car exhaust.

For while I love things new and shiny, I have a deep appreciation for places that had their shiny worn down and thread-bare. Worn down to realness and sheer enough to see through to a just-rolled-out-of-bed self. Those are the places for all people. For people unwelcome in shinier places. People who are different, whose islands of refuge are constantly shrinking and shifting.

As I walk today I think of what I love about the Mission. The Mission I remember is a place of welcome to people familiar with being unwelcome. I think about the impoverished, the immigrants or even refugees from a more domestic, yet hostile way of life, trying to eke out a small space of comfort. I think about the homeless and how they are unwelcome not only in neighborhoods, but sidewalks, parks and underpasses. Where next?

As I walk down Mission and then Valencia, I feel compelled to capture its essence before it is gone. There seems to be a pattern between alternating old with new. I linger at older established businesses and look at the bumpy lacquer of tape melded to the window, competing with the cloudy patina of handprints. These are the handprints of real people who once belonged there.

I wonder...where will all these people go?

BETRAY

Which part of me should I betray
By denying my ancestors
The part of me with browner skin
Or the one you see outside

Even my own government
Asks me to choose between
And makes me check a box
That doesn't even describe me

The box says Asian
The box says African American
The box says Hispanic
The box says Caucasian, (not Hispanic)

And each side says
You are one of us
You are none of us
They are both right and wrong

I hardly speak the language
But it feels good on my tongue

And I know many customs
And yet don't quite fit in

And the me you want to see
Masks something deeper
And makes me privy to thoughts
You would never say if you knew

I'm not food spices and music
Or merely a flesh tone
But a life of cultural wealth
And a sense of belonging

I feel richer for both
And not less than each
But if I really must choose
I am Latinx

LA CHINA POBLANA IN PANORAMA CITY

The streetlight blinks reluctantly in Panorama City
And La China is nowhere to be found
Not in the movie theater or billboard
Not in Sunday service

I first met her in the kitchen
Over tea and stories
I believed you just a fairy tale then
The hero princess of my childhood

She broke free of men
Denouncing wealth
Clinging to her culture
With the craft of women

Whether we cook or weave
Embroider or sew
Magic threading every stitch
Mother to daughter to granddaughter

My inheritance cannot be taxed

Sewing, planting, harvesting
Poultices and teas
Prayers and candles

Cactus gardens bloom, magic
Yerba Buena tea, magic
Poems and family story, magic
Singing, dancing, creating, magic

I know why you left this place
They drove you out with fancy coffee
So you left in each moving box
Linked to people not place

La China, we went to Puebla
To visit you, pay respects
But you were not there
They again enslaved you

You were sent from home
Across the world
And found your sanctuary
With women

I thought I lost you
When I lost my her
My grandma's community erased
Then, I remembered my inheritance

HER NAME IS RAGE

You pretend she isn't there
Hide her from polite company
Wall her away in some secret cell
Deny her existence, but she is there
Not cowering in the dark, but waiting
Waiting for a chance to break free
To break free and burn the city down
Take you and everything with it
She'll burn you with her acid breath
Breathe fire, spit venom
And her name? Her name is Rage
And she has been waiting
Waiting lifetimes to break the cycle
To scream the truth
Incinerate the ignorant
Crush the complicit
Destroy the deniers
Savor the destruction of the unsavory
Savor the flicker of recognition
As they realize their mistake
The mistake of believing that children stay small
Stay weak or scared

Stay intimidated
Stay stuck and afraid
Stay powerless
Until they meet her, Rage
Rage is patient, taking her time
Striking when the predator turns prey
They are so slow to realize
The shift of power
They can hardly remember handing over the scepter
Like a has-been celebrity
Whose enabler fans make them cling to days of glory
Days of power, days of control
Control over others
A diminutive kingdom
Of terrorized children
Who don't. Stay. Small
Some don't stay afraid
Some meet Rage
And some become her
Others lock her up
Still more let her out
And the exoskeletal, damaged ones

Who take food from their own mouths to feed her
Give her strength
Strength to finish the fight and win
And she will win, Rage
She is a stoked fire
Well fed and cared for
She is waiting
For that small flicker of recognition
When the predator realizes it's the prey

SOMETHING ANCIENT

Luna Madre, incandescent and luminous
Bathe in Khepra's morning light
Stand protected in Udjat's watchful eye
Where cobra and vulture do angels bide
Of mother earth and father sky

Arachnid granddaughter given signs
Of scarab announcing, I'm here
And vulture's beauty of goddess making
To rule the valley of the kings
And Luna Madre keeps peace in the valley

Where Golden Dawn is not first light
But ghastly and macabre rite
Sacred essence consumed by all
Til dread of moon seeps in the soul
And only planets save or feed

In darker places, hearts don't rest
But beating in and out of chest
Call Mercury to summon Michael
Opening celestial doors to all

A door the conduit cannot shut

Call on something ancient
Something she rocked in cradle with
Who shares the language and ritual
Where familiarity is safer than safety
Safer in the airless in between

Alpha et Omega
Alpha et Omega
Again and again and again
Where programming is thwarted
By an unplugged cord

A cord cut by deprogramming
Unraveling, unsettling,
Unapologetic, unmerciful
Unbecoming and unrelenting
A torrent of earth, water, fire, air, spirit

Till carnelian, lapis, malachite, obsidian
A rainbow of sunstone, quartz and calcite

May they speak to the soil and flowers and trees
Sing skyward at the top of their lungs
Imploring Luna Madre to spare them

Just this once

SHIPWRECK,
(A SURVIVOR'S STORY)

What speaks of heart-fatigue?
A heaviness too much to carry
A burden of tired ventricles
A slowing beat, softer, quieter
A minimal compliancy
That qualifies as life
But perhaps not living
Of heaving to higher ground
Thrashing through angry surf
To exhaust, collapse
To a faraway slumber
Despite the pummel
Of wave after wave
Many stay here
This soft-sand bedding
This place above drowning
Offers very little comfort
Most would recognize
But to those of us
Who feel safer in elements
Relaxed in danger's proximity

Would paint our paradise
In the color of a bruise
Purple, green, red
And the ugly yellow
Of an arnica bath
Drawn by an imaginary love
That promises healing
With a soft voice and loving arms
And instead, we eat our crumbs
Grateful, and drink the salty waves of tears
Send our SOSs to no one
And repeat the mantra
I'm fine, I'm fine
Occasionally, we open our eyes
In the sunlight, we see above shore
See the quiet forest beyond
Push our heart-weary selves up
And move beyond this place

AS MY FOOTHOLD CRUMBLES

As my foothold crumbles
And terra non firma
Flow in rivulets swaying
Bounce down the hillside
Spill and fall to polish rock
Beacon me release and flow
Let go
Let go
Let go
Let gravity relieve the burden
Release
Release
Release
This package you carry
This thing you don't need
That you clutch to your chest
Owns your body
But never your soul
Release
Release
Release
Leave it here on the hill
The loss of purchase
Is the way out

THE SENTRIES VIEW

Somber, sombre looking down
Furtive tendrils, wrapping round
Feeding and fattening fears
As I try to discern the sound
That soft scrape of leathery wings
That scurry of something unwelcome
And I try to summon dragons
But only call on daemons
And whisper
And then they
But I try to
But can't, can't breathe
As they turn to me and smile
Say, *do you want to talk?*
Keep them company?
And I look at them
And they at me
I see their pain
The pain of exile
That they must see in me
For a moment we just gaze
And wonder at this odd connection
They speak again to me and say

Dance with me
And we join hands
And begin to spin
This feels familiar
And safe, so we swirl
We spin and glide
Until we are giddy and fall back
We land softly and laugh
As I look back to say thank you
I see only my reflection

Reflection...look in the mirror
There are always green eyes
But sometimes not yours
Another voice or body
Agender or femme

DOWN THE FOGGY STREETS OF MY MIND 2

Down the foggy streets of my mind
I disappear
In blissful insignificance
Imbibed with invisibility
Calmed by this camouflage
Alone in anonymity
Follow familiar trails
Like walking in the dark
In the welcome desolation
This place I call home
Weaving through shadow
With shadow
Tinted lavender and taupe
With delicate brush strokes
Making swirling spirals
Of mosses and cool water
Where you think you see me
But not I you
My eyes see places that once existed
Never existed
Not yet
Where sound vibrates energy

Rattling cells and pulsing blood
Blood begins in waterfalls and rapids
And slows to quiet pools
That vibrate to the beat
Of soft ripples
That vibrate in patterns of time
That comes in wavelengths
Being slower or faster
Or doesn't exist
And the ground not up or down
But undulating, pulsating
This place is vast
Just and inch away
Takes less than one step
But sound travels poorly
and light seems to bend
To allow ancient senses
To awake and arise
And commune with spirit
The gift of stories
By the firelight of stars
A fountain of spark and sparkle
A ray of moonlight

Slipping under the water
Eyes adjusting, lungs adjusting
Stay a little longer
Each time a little longer
And maybe not return

MY CONSTANT

As you were leaving I grabbed a tendril-specter of you that I stashed away.

I keep her as my talisman and her name is my mantra.

I use them when the first world becomes unbearable and I retreat to
the other.

She blithely brushes away the ugliness in ways acid and sandpaper could not.

I keep her close and safely tucked away.

She is my constant.

She keeps me from floating to the other, inner world where

I feel most at home.

I glide between two worlds never really belonging to either.

And I only fully lived in that first world, when she was still there.

A PINT OF INDIGO

Every heart has a quiet nest
A tiny pocket of pain
Chamber of purple and indigo
Coursing to the beat

For unless exposed,
Blood isn't really red
Those delicate things
Unexposed can't bleed or hurt

So, keep safe that secret self
Internal voyeur, cinephile
Hush her whispers
To unworthy ears

Nestle her deeply into the chest
Tuck her into quilts and down
Pull the blinds for dark and rest
May she stay safe and sound

THE SACRED IN BETWEEN

There are certain things we hold
in the spaces in between us
The warm energy that passes
Back and forth
Like a circuit, like a flow
Embraces us
In our sacred circle
Of love and heat
Eternal bonds
Stronger than gravity
We are unrestrained
We are the mysteries
Of the universe, of the divine
And I seek only...
The tiny truths
The slow unwrapping of trust
The cemented bondings
Of love as a verb
And quiet knowledge

That we have eternity
To fuel this flame

IN A LANGUAGE ALL MY OWN

In a language all my own
I can see my words
With subtle hues
And strong lines

In a language all my own
I can taste the letters
And smell the sentences
And they nourish me

I see nuances in words
Like colors of synesthesia
Like the feeling of chords
Not auditory, but tactile

When the bass synchronizes
With your heart beat
Like a musical pacemaker
Conducting at its will

Veil that obscures vision
In momentary sightlessness

Of bright intensity
Not seen, but experienced

Warming on the inside
Without touching the outsight
Entering the soul
Only through orbs
Feeling of numbness
Ecstatic oneness
Not warm or cold, but only just
In a language all my own

I live

WHAT KIND OF MAGIC?

What could make beauty appear?
In an oasis, a mirage
What kind of spell
Could turn a desert green?
Dense, aquatic, lush
What trick of the eye
Could make you see the future?
Sensual and sensing
How long does a tree
Have to wait for the rain?
Before it's green turns gray
If a heart is full
Of a different love
Does it struggle with the beat?
What if we chase hunger
But are dying of thirst?
While a river at our feet
Could hunger be a language, primal?
A baby cries, a hunter yells
And we feed and feed
Til our stomachs are full
But hearts and souls echo

Echo the loneliness and emptiness
Of a forgotten and desolate place
Of loose gravel and unsteady footing
Of the winds of disorientation
Of the fragility of being lost
Of the knowing that no one is searching
Or maybe one tiny light
With no promise or certainty
Just company of an unmapped journey
Just I see you, do you see me?
What if we just agreed
To walk a while, talk a while
Fellow travelers on this short road
And if one had the need to feed?
Could take another trail
A trail to feast until satiated
And returned to this road
Ready to drink

INNER VOICE

The tongue knows few words
That can capture what's unknown
And falters with ephemera
Because the letters are too round
Or slippery
Because the words are hard to swallow
Or jagged
Because words that live outside
Are too rugged
Because the language of inside
Is too crystalline
Too delicate to be moved around
Too ethereal to be held
Too alien to be understood

FEAST OF
TRAUMAVERSARY

On this shortest day
In this place that I do not belong
I see wings clipped, feathers plucked
Bird made flightless before flight
And uses its will to create lift
To escape just before

On this shortest day
I send light under wings
Make light, make lightness
Make lighter and loftier
Before fleeing, unseen by
And revealed in lunar luminescence

Stepping into alternate realm
Watching, waiting
Waiting for a sign of safety
Waiting for my human green card
Waiting for an invitation
That never comes, never comes

Lunar light like tidal push-pull
Beckons and repels
Promises and poisons
Revere and repulses
So visceral, vain and violent

As only deities can do

THE GRAND FINALE, PART 2*

I remember parking on the railroad track
Somewhere in Newhall
To avoid going home
Getting dumped on my birthday
My seventeenth birthday
Only a few days before getting robbed
A cold knife at my throat
Not the first or last violent birthday
And the shitty poem
My suicide note
Matched my mood, shitty
Bored after an hour
I drove back home
Home, the place I'd avoided
Shunned for the Manager's office in a nightclub
Preferring anywhere, but my origins
Running from the lost love of a damaged girl
Who traded my story for kindness
Who preferred the attention of sex work for love
Who I rescued over and over again
Only to be replaced by those more tenuous

Those less loyal
She used me for her cause
It started slowly, the looks, the stares
The comments, the laughs
The pointing whispers
The, *you deserved it*
The , *Slut and Whore*
I can't go anywhere
I can't believe this
I was just raped
The bullseye, the target
The suffocating scrutiny
I want invisibility
I need isolation
Just stop looking at me

Do you want to hear a story?
It is about the girl who got away

*The first Grand Finale was a suicide note

THE POET WHO

The Poet That Who?
Most of us want to be immortalized
Be published and validated
Win awards and be best sellers
Get into the in crowds
Me? Some part of me wants that too.
But my reward? My reward is in the truth.
The unearthing of secrets

I am not the pretty word poet
I am not the academic poet
I'm a survivor, a street urchin
My story isn't pretty
I'm not dressing it up
I'm not trying to make you like me
I'm just trying to be real

My reward is the person who tells me
Tells me the untold story
Of 20, 40, 60+ years ago
The story the spouse doesn't know
Of the pretty word poet who unburdens

Lets the terrifying truth out
Amplified to intimate strangers

At first the words are shaky
Voice and hands tremble
I translate the trembling
No story spine, hero's journey
Here the protagonist licks mortal wounds
Wounds that cells survive, but the soul
The soul, much less so

And the searching eyes that wonder
Do you see me? And, I *say yes*
And in that recognition, sigh of relief
They said, *I knew I could do it because you were here*
And in that moment, I affirm my purpose
This is not for me, but for all of us
Those of us sacrificed by gluttonous greed

SOLITUDE

I find comfort in solitude
It's misunderstood
Often mistaken for loneliness
It's not the same

Loneliness Is a vacant crater
Solitude is different

Quiet conversation with yourself
Being alone
But not feeling alone
A comfortable quiet

Where the outspoken word is unwelcome
And would shatter the calm stillness

Quiet as its own language
One understood only by the speaker-listener
As one and the same
One's own true first language

I speak it well
And do not pass it on to others

The part of me that is not shared
Spoken here in the code of poetry
Seen, not felt by others
As they would see their green, and not mine

Practice your language
For therein lies all the answers
Answers true and just
 As if given to you by some higher power

And perhaps it is
Quiet conversations with you and your god

Some call it conscience
Others inner self
Call it what you like

I have my own name
And I keep it to myself

THE NIGHT SHIFT

The night shift begins
As I long to rest
To the soft buzz of traffic
Hastens my fog
Which welcomes me in
As BART softly calls
To those still awake
And I board those sounds
To take me away
While my dog softly snores
And I sit alone in darkness
And watch the blinking lights
That move across the bridge
Send me messages
Send messages of hope
That day will come soon
That danger can't find me
I slowly drift
As the fridge hums a lullaby
Made just for me
I slowly drift
And let things be...

EXIT DOOR

Right this way
Don't make a sound
Just keep moving
You've made it through
Stay to the left
Out of the light
Once to the door?
Run
You made it out
This is the beginning

READING GUIDE

Theme: **Numbness vs Being Fully Present**

Have you ever felt your emotions shut down or feel disconnected from yourself? This is a form of dissociation. We all do it a little bit, sometimes going on autopilot. Highway hypnosis is like that, where you know you were driving, but not fully present. How are you feeling right now? Notice whether you feel hot, cold, happy, bored. Now, just notice it without judgement.

When we feel unsafe or experience trauma, the brain gets better and better at keeping the worst details from us. This is so we can carry on with our daily activities. Sometimes those memories sneak out unexpectedly. This is known as a flashback. Flashbacks can be auditory, (sound), visual, (seeing) or somatic, (body sensation). They can feel so real as if it is happening now. Think of it as pressure release. Flashbacks are usually triggered by sounds like sirens, a certain time of the day or even a tv show or song.

If it is serious enough, you can get a Dissociative Disorder. The most common Dissociative Disorder is PTSD, Post Traumatic Stress Disorder. Being around violence or growing up in an unsafe home can cause this. If you don't feel safe, talking to a school counselor can help get you support.

Also, if you feel like you are in crisis, text 741741. Someone will text you back and help you in that moment. Please find a safe adult to tell. And know that in the moment the feelings are overwhelming, but if you can just pause and wait til morning or later, it will soften.

We've been trained to believe that people with mental disorders are dangerous, lazy, unstable etc. This isn't true and the number one cause is trauma. In every classroom, office, family or city, ¼ of the population deals with mental illness or addiction. And those who are not surviving it well deserve to be safe and have basic human rights just as much as people who have had support to learn how to manage it better. No matter if you have a diagnosis or not, life can be rewarding, you can follow your passion and be your authentic self.

Prompt:
Think of a time in life where you felt unsafe but were afraid to tell someone.

Use the prompt to create a poem giving yourself a hopeful message. In your poem make sure to tell yourself that you deserve to feel safe.

Say it to yourself out loud, "I deserve to feel safe". Remember, there is NOTHING you can ever do that would make you deserve to have ANY harm done to you. You deserve to feel safe, even if you are being unsafe. Read your poem out loud to remind yourself how deserving of goodness you are.

If you live with a mental disorder or illness, it means you can survive a lot. If this was a comic book story, you would have superhuman powers!

Representative Poems

ACKNOWLEDGMENTS

This has been an amazing healing journey and I am lucky to have so much support from the Bay Area poetry community. As poets, we are empaths and many of us have a trauma story to tell. Though our hearts might be broken we haven't stopped dreaming.

I am blessed to have both my sister Jenny and best friend of 54 years, Hannah love and accept me for who I am. My mom who believed me when I first started to come forward about some of the abuse I had endured. Being believed is critical to healing. Kisses and love to my two wonderful children, who have had an adventurous life with their quirky mom. I also want to acknowledge my great grandmother Manosa, on my dad's side. Like many women at the turn of the last century, she spent the last decades of her life in an institution and I hope to someday, discover why.

I have so many writers that I have learned from and been inspired by, the list is enormous. The generosity among those who commune together in the church of words cannot be understated. Being unique, authentic and true to yourself is celebrated and welcomed here.

I was dusted with moon magic by MK Chavez, my amazing editor. She infuses beauty into everything she touches and her gentle guidance was both nurturing and visionary. Of course this story could not be possible without the support and belief from J. K. Fowler and Nomadic Press for always giving voice to those unheard or misunderstood voices,

I wholeheartedly support their mission. From the moment I went to my first Nomadic Press event, I knew this is where I wanted to be.

I'd like to acknowledge the following presses, who first gave voice to this work. The following anthologies list previously published work:

Have you Heard Us Yet, Abrams Claghorn Gallery (2018) "While the World Sleeps"
Poetry Expressed (2018) "The Abyss"
Collosus Home (2020) "Morning Mission Musings"

Kelliane Parker

Kelliane Parker is a Queer, Latinx, Bay Area Poet. Kelliane was first diagnosed with what is now called DID in 1991. She is a survivor of ritual and childhood sexual abuse, sexual assault, and domestic violence. In her own words, she unearths secrets and deconstructs stories about surviving sexual, physical, and emotional violence. Her mission is to end the stigma of shame and blame that survivors face. Kelliane can be found educating audiences about PTSD, DID, and other dissociative disorders caused by trauma by others. She is a regular feature in the Bay Area poetry scene and is the co-host of My Word Open Mic in Berkeley, California. She can be found at kellianeparkerpoetry.com.

OTHER WAYS TO SUPPORT NOMADIC PRESS' WRITERS

In 2020, two funds geared specifically toward supporting our writers were created: the **Nomadic Press Black Writers Fund** and the **Nomadic Press Emergency Fund**.

The former is a forever fund that puts money directly into the pockets of our Black writers. The latter provides dignity-centered emergency grants to any of our writers in need.

Please consider supporting these funds. You can also more generally support Nomadic Press by donating to our general fund via nomadicpress.org/donate and by continuing to buy our books. As always, thank you for your support!

Scan below for more information and/or to donate.
You can also donate at nomadicpress.org/store.